WORLD IN
FOCUS

FOCUS ON
Brazil

SIMON SCOONES

WORLD ALMANAC® LIBRARY

Please visit our web site at: www.worldalmanaclibrary.com
For a free color catalog describing World Almanac® Library's list of high-quality books
and multimedia programs, call 1-800-848-2928 (USA) or 1-800-387-3178 (Canada).
World Almanac® Library's fax: (414) 332-3567.

Library of Congress Cataloging-in-Publication Data

Scoones, Simon.
    Focus on Brazil / by Simon Scoones.
        p. cm. — (World in focus)
    Includes bibliographical references and index.
    ISBN 0-8368-6720-3 (lib. bdg.)
    ISBN 0-8368-6727-0 (softcover)
    1. Brazil—Juvenile literature. 2. Brazil—Textbooks. I. Title. II. World in focus
(Milwaukee, Wis.)
    F2508.5.S386   2007
    981—dc22   2006001922

This North American edition first published in 2007 by
World Almanac® Library
A Member of the WRC Media Family of Companies
330 West Olive Street, Suite 100
Milwaukee, WI 53212 USA

This U.S. edition copyright © 2007 by World Almanac® Library. Original edition copyright
© 2006 by Hodder Wayland. First published in 2006 by Hodder Wayland, an imprint of
Hodder Children's Books, a division of Hodder Headline Limited, 338 Euston Road,
London NW1 3BH, U.K.

Commissioning editor: Victoria Brooker
Editor: Nicola Barber
Inside design: Chris Halls, www.mindseyedesign.co.uk
Cover design: Hodder Wayland
Series concept and project management by EASI-Educational Resourcing (info@easi-er.co.uk)
Statistical research: Anna Bowden
Maps and graphs: Martin Darlison, Encompass Graphics

World Almanac® Library editors: Alan Wachtel and Leifa Butrick
World Almanac® Library cover design: Scott Krall

Picture acknowledgements: The author and publisher would like to thank the following for allowing
their pictures to be reproduced in this publication: Corbis title page (Ricardo Azoury), 9 (Stapleton
Collection), 11 (Historical Picture Archive), 13 (Ricardo Azoury), 23 (Reuters), 25 (Adriano
Machado/Reuters), 36 (Mariana Bazo/Reuters), 37 (Ammar Awad/Reuters); Edward Parker/Images
Everything Limited 4, 6, 7, 8, 10, 12, 14, 15, 16, 17, 18, 20, 21, 22, 24, 26 (World Wildlife Fund),
27, 28, 29 (World Wildlife Fund), 30 (World Wildlife Fund), 31, 32, 33, 34, 38, 39, 40, 41, 42, 43,
44, 46, 47, 48, 49, 50, 51, 52, 53, 54, 55, 56, 57, 58, 59.

The data used to produce the graphics and data panels in this title were the latest available at the
time of production.

Printed in China

1 2 3 4 5 6 7 8 9 10 09 08 07 06

CONTENTS

Cover: Young women beat the rhythm of the samba on the drums during Carnival.

Title page: Parades are a big part of Carnival in Brazil

CHAPTER 1

Brazil –
An Overview

Covering more than half of South America, Brazil is the world's fifth largest country. It is so big that it spreads across four time zones, and the distance from its eastern coast to its western boundaries is as great as from New York to Los Angeles.

FERTILE COUNTRY

No other country has so much fresh water. The Amazon River has the largest volume in the world, carrying 20 percent of all the world's river water. The Amazon River basin covers more than 1,930,000 square miles (5 million square kilometers) over nine countries, and contains the biggest expanse of rain forest on the planet. Three other vast rivers—the Paraná, the Paraguai, and the São Francisco—wind their way across Brazil. The country's farmland is rich, with ample rainfall in many parts of the country and large areas of fertile soil that produce most of the world's coffee and bumper crops of sugar cane, soy beans, and cocoa. Vast cattle ranches sprawl across the countryside. Brazil is also a major industrial power. Brazilians make many goods, including steel, cars, computers, and even TV programs that are sold all over the world.

▼ At the Brazil-Argentina border, 275 waterfalls cascade over a precipice nearly 2 miles (3 km) wide to create the Iguaçú Falls, one of the biggest waterfalls in the world.

Focus on: Brazilwood

Some people say that Brazil got its name from a kind of redwood tree called *pau brasil*, or brazilwood, that grows on the coast. Amerindians once used the red sap from brazilwood trees as makeup. In 1501, the Portuguese sent Amerigo Vespucci, an Italian explorer, to Brazil. Vespucci returned to Europe with a bulging cargo of brazilwood. The Portuguese used the sap from the brazilwood as dye. Today, brazilwood trees still grow in the forests along Brazil's coastal strip, although much of this Atlantic forest environment has been destroyed.

▶ Brazilwood dye, produced from the sap of the tree, is still used to make high-quality red inks.

THE PEOPLE OF BRAZIL

Brazilians themselves are as varied as their country's landscape. Although Amerindians are the original Brazilians, over the last five hundred years, immigrants have come from every corner of the globe to make their home in Brazil. Most of today's 180.7 million Brazilians speak Portuguese as their main language. Portuguese-style buildings and churches still stand as reminders of the three centuries that Brazil was Portugal's most important colony. From the party atmosphere of the annual Carnival to the mysterious depths of the Amazon basin, Brazil is a fascinating country full of contrasts.

Physical Geography

- 🗁 Land area: 3,265,059 square miles/ 8,456,510 square km
- 🗁 Water area: 21,411 sq miles/55,455 sq km
- 🗁 Total area: 3,286,470 sq miles/8,511,965 sq km
- 🗁 World rank (by area): 5
- 🗁 Land boundaries: 9,123 miles/14,691 km
- 🗁 Border countries: Argentina, Bolivia, Colombia, French Guiana, Guiana, Paraguay, Peru, Suriname, Uruguay, Venezuela
- 🗁 Coastline: 4,652 miles/7,491 km
- 🗁 Highest point: Pico da Neblina (9,888 feet/3,014 meters)
- 🗁 Lowest point: Atlantic Ocean (0 ft/0 m)

Source: CIA World Factbook

▲ A huge crowd gathers in Salvador, capital of the northeastern state of Bahia, to celebrate Independence Day on September 7. On this day in 1822, Brazil became independent from Portugal.

? Did You Know?

Brazil borders every other South American country except Chile and Ecuador.

◄ The colors of Brazil's national flag have special meanings. The green stands for land and forest, the yellow for the country's gold, and the blue for its stunning blue skies.

CHAPTER 2

History

Thousands of years ago, the first American peoples moved slowly south in search of new hunting grounds and warmer climates. Archaeologists believe that people came down from the Andes mountain range into the Brazilian lowlands and the Amazon basin around 10,000 BC. Most early signs of life have long since rotted away in the tropical heat, but pieces of pottery and human remains have been found in a cave in the Amazon rain forest at Monte Alegre. The cave walls are decorated with paintings of human and animal figures, giving an idea of what life was like in those early times.

THE ORIGINAL BRAZILIANS

The earliest inhabitants of Brazil's tropical lowlands are collectively known as Amerindians. Groups of Amerindians developed their own ways of life, moving from place to place to hunt game and gather fruits from the forest. Along the Amazon's riverbanks, the Amerindians kept turtles in pens. Later they would eat the turtle meat and carve their shells into tools.

MOVING TO THE COAST

Around 7000 BC, some Amerindian groups moved eastward to escape the high temperatures inland. Gradually, people settled in villages along Brazil's coastal strip. One of the biggest of these groups was the Tupinambá.

▼ Cave art on the Pedra da Concha (Shell Rock) in Catimbau National Park, northeast Brazil, dates back more than 6,000 years. By studying the cave paintings of northeast Brazil, archaeologists believe that the earliest Brazilians in this region hunted large game with pointed stone spears.

◀ This engraving of 1557 illustrates the story of a German soldier, Hans Staden, who traveled to Brazil on a Portuguese ship in 1549. He was shipwrecked and then captured by the Tupinambá, who threatened to kill and eat him. After some months in captivity, Staden escaped unharmed.

The Tupinambá (Tupi) grew crops such as yams, sweet potatoes, and tobacco and lived in large, thatched houses that held as many as thirty families each. They were also cannibals. After much singing and dancing, they celebrated the capture of their enemies by eating them. Many towns along the coast still have Tupi names.

Unlike the great ancient civilizations of the Maya in Central America and the Incas further to the west and south in South America, no single group controlled ancient Brazil. Yet, by the time the Europeans arrived in the 1500s, as many as six million Amerindians lived in the country in thousands of groups, each one with its own traditions and customs. Many of these groups have survived to the present.

Focus on: Ancient Shellfish Eaters

Marajó island lies near the mouth of the Amazon River. About 3,000 years ago on Marajó, the Annatuba people ate shellfish and built great mounds out of their shells, known as *sambaquis*. Some *sambaquis* were used as houses. Others became graveyards where the dead were buried with some of their personal belongings.

 Did You Know?

Despite the hot, steamy environment, the earliest inhabitants of the Amazon basin wore long tunics down to their ankles. These garments helped protect them from biting insects.

DISCOVERY BY MISTAKE

After the European "discovery" of the Americas in 1492, the Spanish and Portuguese signed an agreement in 1494 that allowed the Portuguese to claim the territory that makes up modern-day Brazil. Although Brazil later became Portugal's biggest colony, the Portuguese did not actually arrive in the country until 1500—and that was by mistake! In that year, King Emmanuel of Portugal instructed Pedro Álvares Cabral, a talented explorer, to command a fleet of thirteen ships and 1,200 men. The king told Cabral to travel the world to introduce Christianity wherever he went—by force if necessary. Cabral left Portugal on March 9, 1500, but his fleet was blown off course as it sailed around Africa and was swept by ocean currents across the Atlantic. On April 25, Cabral spotted land, which he thought was part of an island. Cabral had actually reached what is now Brazil, near the town of Porto Seguro.

Focus on: São Paulo

São Paulo was just a cluster of mud houses in the 1500s when two Jesuit priests set up a mission and a school to spread the Catholic message. The town grew as Portuguese explorers, known as *bandeirantes*, used it as a stopover before venturing further into Brazil's interior. It was not until the late 1900s, however, that São Paulo became a city, thanks to the boom in the coffee business. Thousands of immigrants from Italy, Spain, Japan, Syria, and Lebanon came to work on the coffee plantations, and the coffee barons became increasingly wealthy.

▼ At Coroa Vermelha, north of Porto Seguro, a cross marks the spot where Cabral and his men first set foot on South American soil in 1500.

Cabral and his men resumed their voyage to Africa and India, but more Portuguese expeditions to Brazil followed. On New Year's Day 1502, three ships under the command of Amerigo Vespucci, reached a narrow opening in the coastline surrounded by mountains. Beyond lay a body of water that Vespucci guessed was the mouth of a river. In fact, it was a beautiful bay dotted with islands, called Guanabara (or "arm of the sea") by the Amerindian Tamoio people who lived there. Despite his mistake, Vespucci named this stretch of water "the river of January." The name stuck, and the city built on the bay was named Rio de Janeiro.

SWEAT AND TOIL

Portugal's control over Brazil strengthened as Portuguese merchants established outposts along the coast. At first, the Amerindians traded *pau brasil* wood with the Portuguese, but relations soured after the European invaders forced the natives to work on sugar plantations. As the plantations multiplied, the Portuguese imported black people from West Africa to provide slave labor. Work on the sugar plantations was brutal. Most plantation slaves only lasted eight years. More slaves were imported and forced to work on coffee plantations and in the diamond and gold mines. It was the sweat and toil of these slaves that turned Brazil into Portugal's richest colony.

▲ This painting from the 1830s shows African slaves washing diamonds under the watchful eyes of their Portuguese slave drivers.

 Did You Know?

Between 1502 and 1870, more than 3.5 million Africans were exported as slaves to Brazil, nearly six times the number shipped to the United States during the same time.

THE CRUMBLING COLONY

When French armies under Napoléon Bonaparte invaded Portugal in 1807, the Portuguese royal family moved to the safety of Brazil. This was the only time a European nation was ruled from across the Atlantic Ocean. Although the king moved back in 1820, his son, Dom Pedro stayed in Brazil. Two years later, Dom Pedro declared Brazil's independence from Portugal. Not wanting to take his father's title of king, Dom Pedro became the first emperor of Brazil.

AN END TO THE MONARCHY

As emperor, Dom Pedro found it difficult to keep the peace. Many of his subjects wanted Brazil to remain under Portuguese rule. Under Dom Pedro's command, Brazil also lost a war with Argentina over territory in the south that later became the republic of Uruguay. After ten troubled years, Dom Pedro was forced to abdicate. He returned to Portugal in 1826. His son, Pedro II, replaced him as emperor in 1831. He was just five years old. Pedro II's reign was peaceful and prosperous, lasting more than half a century. He gave ordinary Brazilians more freedom and gradually phased out slavery, abolishing it altogether in 1888. During his reign, Brazil also took the first steps toward industrialization with the introduction of the steam engine and the construction of the country's first paved roads. Pedro II was a

Focus on: The First Freedom Fighter

In the late 1700s, the Portuguese used the gold from the state of Minas Gerais in Brazil to pay for their war against Napoleon. The gold mines were running out of gold, however, so the Portuguese taxed the miners' declining gold supply to make up the difference. In 1789, a dentist, Joaquim José da Silva Xavier, nicknamed "Tiradentes" (or "tooth puller"), led protests against the Portuguese. Tiradentes was eventually captured and executed on April 21, 1792. His head and pieces of his body were displayed for all to see to prevent another uprising. Today, April 21 is a national holiday in Brazil to remember Tiradentes, one of the country's bravest heroes.

▶ A statue of a bearded, long-haired Tiradentes stands outside the Palácio Tiradentes in Rio. The Palácio is on the site of the jail where Tiradentes spent his last days.

popular leader. Nevertheless, some thought that he was not liberal enough, while others, like the slave owners, disapproved of his reforms. In 1889, the military organized a coup to replace Pedro II and the royal family with a president and a government elected by the people. In this way, the republic of Brazil was born.

BRUTAL RULE

During the early years of the republic, the coffee barons and other rich merchants in São Paulo and Minas Gerais were very powerful. Many of them ruled their workers like dictators. In 1930, a cattle rancher, Getúlio Vargas, became president. To shift power away from the coffee barons of São Paulo, Vargas passed new laws that gave people the right to support the political party of their choice. To help poorer Brazilians, he introduced social security and a minimum wage. Under constant pressure from his opponents, however, Vargas became more dictatorial. Vargas was thrown out of office in 1945, but he became president again in 1950. Corruption scandals forced him out for a second time just four years later. Soon after, Vargas committed suicide.

A group of generals seized power in 1964. They banned political parties, and their opponents faced violence and torture in detention camps. More than twenty years later, massive foreign debts and growing unrest finally persuaded the military dictators to step aside and allow people to choose their own government. Brazil's problems didn't end, however, because debt and inflation continued to spiral out of control. In 1994, with the biggest election victory in forty years, President Fernando Henrique Cardoso began to put the Brazilian economy back on track and to tackle the many problems of the Brazilian poor. In 2002, after two terms in office, Cardoso gave up the presidency. President Luis Inácio Lula da Silva replaced Cardoso and continues to govern Brazil today.

▼ As president, Lula da Silva has made a point of connecting with ordinary Brazilians—a very different style of leadership from that of Brazil's past rulers.

CHAPTER 3

Landscape and Climate

Many people believe Brazil is a country covered by hot, humid rain forest. While this is true for one-third of the country, temperatures and rainfall vary from region to region. Outside the tropics, some southern parts of Brazil even get a dusting of snow in the winter months. Although Brazil has no snow-capped mountains, deserts, or volcanoes, the country can boast a great range of landscapes thanks to large variations in its climate.

FLOODED FORESTS

The climate in the Amazon basin is equatorial, with hot sunshine and more than 79 inches (2,000 millimeters) of rain a year. Much of this water drains into the Amazon river and its tributaries that wind their way toward the Brazilian coast. The hot, wet conditions enable plants and trees to grow every day of the year, creating the world's largest area of rain forest. Some of the land, known as *várzea*, is so low that it is often flooded.

Focus on: The Valley of the Dinosaurs

Brazil's highest mountains are in the north, near the border with Venezuela. The mountains form part of the Guiana Shield, a vast shelf of sedimentary rock more than two billion years old. The Guiana Shield was part of a huge continent called Gondwanaland before movements of Earth's plates split up the continent to create South America and Africa. In the northeastern state of Paraíba, fossilized dinosaur tracks are etched into the ground, a reminder of the time, about 110 million years ago, when as many as ninety different species of dinosaurs roamed on Earth.

? Did You Know?

From source to mouth, the Amazon is 4,087 miles (6,577 km) long. The last 1,967 miles (3,165 km) of the river's journey to the sea is in Brazil. Rio São Francisco in the northeast is Brazil's second longest river.

▲ A harpoon fisherman hunts fruit-eating fish in the flooded *várzea* of the Amazon region.

WETLANDS

South of the Amazon, along the Paraguai river, is the world's largest area of wetland, the Pantanal. In this region, torrential rain falls during the rainy season, between December and March. In many ways, the Pantanal is like an enormous sponge. During the rainy season, the Paraguai river and its tributaries flood this vast expanse of flat land, turning it into a maze of lakes and islands. When the waters retreat, this wet wilderness dries out and becomes a vast feeding ground for birds and animals.

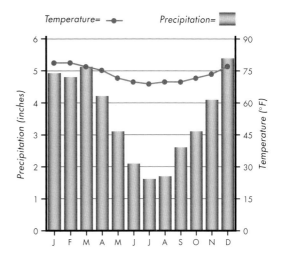

▲ Average monthly climate conditions in Rio de Janeiro

Focus on: Feeding Frenzy in the Wetlands

The Pantanal wetlands are a bird-watcher's paradise. After the rainy season more than 200 species of birds, including the Jabiru stork, come to feed on more than 250 species of fish. Animals such as the giant anteater graze on the water's edge along with thousands of alligators, called caimans. Anacondas like this wet environment, too. These snakes can grow up to 33 feet (10 m) long.

▶ Wading through the Pantanal wetlands, a Jabiru stork looks for mud eels, its favorite meal. Jabiru storks can grow to be more than 4 feet (1.4 m) tall.

THE NORTHEAST

Rainfall is very unreliable in the northeast region. The Trade Winds from the southeast carry moisture from the Atlantic Ocean to the coast but are too weak to bring much rain further inland. Without regular rainfall, much of the northeast has desert-like conditions called *sertão*. Thorny trees, shrubs, and cacti dominate the landscape. Cacti store water in their fleshy trunks, and their waxy skin stops them from losing precious water. When enough rain falls during the short, wet season, farmers grow crops such as corn and beans. During drier years, they raise cattle and goats that feed off the thorny plants and shrubs on the parched ground. Droughts in the region can be disastrous for the people who live there. Some people blame the region's cattle ranchers and cotton farmers for increasing the risk of drought. By clearing the scrub to create more land for farming, they take away the plants that help to hold and store water.

 Did You Know?

In the 1980s, the people of the northeastern region experienced a drought that lasted four years. As many as 700,000 people died from hunger and disease.

Focus on: Shifting Sands

Stretching along the northeast coast is an area that is nicknamed, "the Brazilian Sahara." Here, pristine white sand dunes cover 1,600 square miles (27,000 sq km). When the rains come, between November and March, valleys and hollows in the sand fill with water to create silvery lakes that dot the sandy landscape.

▶ In the breathtaking Lençóis Maranhenses National Park, the wind constantly shifts the vast sand dunes.

ATLANTIC FOREST

Along Brazil's Atlantic coast, moisture from the ocean rises and covers the mountainous slopes with a blanket of water vapor. Trees, surrounded by carpets of mosses and ferns, grow well in this damp, misty climate, and the forest is rich in wildlife. Brazil's entire coastal strip was once covered with Atlantic forest. It stretched 40 miles (64 km) inland in the northeast and 200 miles (320 km) inland in the south. By now, people have cleared much of the forest to build houses, grow crops, or to use the trees as timber.

 Did You Know?

In April 2000, UNESCO declared Brazil's Atlantic forest a World Heritage Site. At that time, only 3 percent of the original 4,500 square miles (12,000 sq km) of forest remained.

▼ In this region in the south of Brazil, large areas of Atlantic forest have been cleared to make way for land to grow crops.

THE CENTRAL PLATEAU

The Central Plateau, an area of tropical grassland or *cerrado,* lies to the south of the Amazon and northeast regions. Covering a fifth of Brazil, the Central Plateau has two seasons—one dry and one wet. Only hardy trees with thick bark can survive the severe dry season, and grasses that grow tall during the wet season cover much of the landscape. Large, flat areas on the Central Plateau have been turned into soy bean fields and cattle ranches.

Focus on: Mud Slides in Rio

Destruction of the Atlantic forest has led to disaster in Rio de Janeiro. Heavy storms in spring sometimes create deadly rivers of mud. Without the trees to stop them, these mud slides cascade down the mountain slopes, engulfing everything in their path. In December 2001, 66 people died when their homes were buried in mud. Since then, people have built crash barriers out of old car tires to halt the mud slides in their tracks. In this way, they are recycling garbage and protecting their homes at the same time.

CHAPTER 4

Population and Settlements

With 180.7 million people, Brazil is the fifth most populated country in the world. The highest concentrations of people are in the south and the southeast, in Brazil's two biggest cities, São Paulo and Rio de Janeiro. Conditions in the Pantanal wetlands in the west and in the dense rain forest of the Amazon are too difficult to support large numbers of people.

POPULATION GROWTH

In the 1940s and 1950s, many Brazilians chose to have large families, with an average of six children. More than half the population was under twenty years old. Most children were expected to work, to help support their families. At the same time, improvements in medical care meant that people began to live longer, so the death rate fell. But with such a high birth rate and a falling death rate, the population grew rapidly, at an average of 3 percent a year. Today, the rate of population growth is much slower—about 1 percent, the same rate as the United States. Birth control methods and family planning advice are widely available, and most families have only two children. Instead of working, most children go to school.

THE AMERINDIAN POPULATION

The ancestors of today's Amerindians lived in Brazil long before the Europeans arrived. Today, about 350,000 Brazilians call themselves Amerindian, while millions of Brazilians have some Amerindian ancestry. The Amerindians live together in groups in a wide range of Brazilian environments, including the Amazon rain forest, the *cerrado* of the Central Plateau, and in the dry northeast.

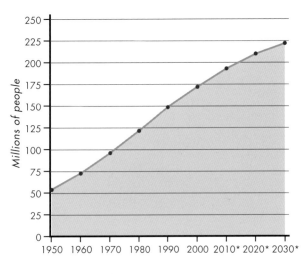

* Projected Population

▲ Population growth 1950-2030

▲ Pataxos Indians are one of the 215 Amerindian groups in Brazil.

Focus on: The Yanomami

One of the largest Amerindian tribes is the Yanomami. Ten thousand Yanomami live in the Amazon rain forest on the border of Brazil and Venezuela. Over generations, the Yanomami have learned how to use rain forest plants and trees without causing lasting damage to the environment. Yanomami culture, however, is under threat. The discovery of gold in Yanomami territory in the 1980s led to pitched battles between Amerindians and gold miners. The outsiders brought diseases with them, such as tuberculosis and malaria, that the Yanomami had not encountered before and to which they had no immunity. Hundreds of Yanomami died. Today, the Yanomami live within a reserve that covers 35,000 square miles (92,000 sq km) to safeguard their future. Without the right to tribal ownership, however, Yanomami are never completely safe.

A government agency called the National Indian Foundation (FUNAI) was set up to defend the interests of Amerindians, and recent presidents have promised to protect Amerindian rights. Brazilian law does not recognize the tribal ownership of land, however. As a result, settlers, miners, or developers for industrial projects or cattle ranches frequently take over Amerindian territory.

THE NEW BRAZILIANS

Since the arrival of the first Europeans more than 500 years ago, waves of immigrants have moved to Brazil to start a new life. As a result, Brazil's population today is extremely diverse. About 53 percent of Brazilians trace their family roots to Europe, 6 percent have ancestors from Africa, and another 38 percent have a mixture of European and African backgrounds. The

mixture of peoples is particularly rich in the northeast. In Salvador da Bahia, descendants of slaves give the city an African feel, and West African influences are apparent in religion, food, clothing, and music in the city.

Other immigrants have also made a mark on the country. Brazil has the largest number of people of Japanese origin outside Japan. Boatloads of Japanese families arrived in the early 1900s to work on coffee plantations in São Paulo state. Many of them stayed, and, today, 1.3 million Brazilians claim Japanese ancestry. Further south, in Santa Catarina state, Blumenau looks and feels like a town in Germany, thanks to the Germans who originally settled there. There is even a beer festival every October to rival the famous beer festival in Munich.

 Did You Know?

Brazil has the world's largest black population outside Africa because nearly half the population have ancestors who were African slaves.

Population Data

- Population: 180.7 million
- Population 0–14 yrs: 28%
- Population 15–64 yrs: 67%
- Population 65+ yrs: 5%
- Population growth rate: 1.2%
- Population density: 55.0 per square mile/ 21.2 per square km
- Urban population: 83%
- Major cities: São Paulo 18,333,000
  Rio de Janeiro 11,469,000
  Belo Horizonte 5,304,000

Source: United Nations and World Bank

THE DRAW OF THE CITY

In the 1970s, cities such as São Paulo, Rio de Janeiro, and Belo Horizonte began swelling in size as people poured in from the surrounding countryside. Poorer families sold their land to rich landowners who created huge soy bean and coffee plantations. At the same time, machines replaced many plantation workers. Farming families in the northeast headed for the cities after their crops were ravaged by severe drought. Many people moved thousands of miles in search of a better life in the city.

Did You Know?

In 1960, 45 percent of Brazil's people lived in towns and cities. By 2003, 83 percent of the population was urban.

Focus on: São Paulo

São Paulo, South America's biggest city, is so large that it has several centers. It resembles a cluster of cities within a city. São Paulo's wealthiest residents live in guarded compounds, and some commute to work in private helicopters that land on heliports on the tops of high-rise buildings. At the other end of the scale, as many as two million people live in *favelas*, slums without basic services such as electricity and running water. The dense concentration of people in one area has a serious environmental impact. A cocktail of pollutants builds up from vehicle exhaust fumes, the fuel burnt in homes, and gases released by the city's many factories. At times, the air in the city is so polluted that many people suffer from stinging eyes and breathing problems.

▲ Luxury apartments and office blocks decorate São Paulo's skyline, and sprawling suburbs spread for miles.

RIO: A TALE OF TWO CITIES

Some residents in Rio live in the most expensive real estate in Brazil. A beachfront apartment can cost millions of dollars. Other families have moved to Barra da Tijuca, Rio's newest neighborhood along the coast. Here, families can bring up their children away from the noise, pollution, and high crime levels of downtown Rio. Barra da Tijuca has wide avenues, department stores, and large, spacious condominium complexes. At the same time, as in other Brazilian cities, many residents live in slums, known as *favelas*.

In Rio, the *favelas* are located on the city's steep hillsides and ravines. The very poorest people live in makeshift buildings and have no running water, electricity, or sewage systems. Growing tensions between drug gangs and the police have made some *favelas* very dangerous places. In April 2004, four thousand armed police were sent into Rio's *favelas* to seize weapons and catch the gang leaders. More than one thousand people died in the street battles that followed. Most of the dead were young black men caught up in the drug trade as a way to make money or support their own drug habits.

IMPROVING THE FAVELAS

Many basic city services would collapse without a workforce from the *favelas*, and *favela* communities tend to look after each other and work hard to find a way out of poverty. To give them a helping hand, Rio's city authorities have been working alongside *favela* dwellers to improve their living conditions. Since 1995, the Favela-Bairro project has been adding facilities such as street lighting, community centers, sewage, and waste disposal systems. By consulting with the people who live there, Favela-Bairro has a chance to bring suitable and lasting improvements to the *favelas*. Favela-Bairro remains the city's most important improvement project, and there are plans to invest another U.S.$1 billion so that more *favelas* will benefit.

BRASÍLIA

In 1960, the government replaced Rio de Janeiro with a new capital city called Brasília, 596 miles (960 km) inland. Brasília's central location was chosen by the Brazilian government to open up the country's Amazon heartland. Many people disliked the move because the new capital was so far away from the centers of population along the coast. Today, Brasília has two million inhabitants, and many people think that it is an outstanding example of a modern, planned city.

 Did You Know?

Roçinha is Rio's oldest and largest *favela*. In the 1950s, Roçinha was just a few makeshift shacks. Today, it has a population of up to 250,000, with its own schools, doctors' offices, fast-food outlets, and Web site. Despite these changes for the better Roçinha hasn't escaped the drug war, and it is estimated that up to U.S.$500,000 worth of drugs goes in and out of Roçinha every week.

◀ The *favela* of Roçinha began in the 1940s, when a group of squatters occupied a hillside in downtown Rio. Today, Roçinha is more like a city within a city.

CHAPTER 5

Government and Politics

In 1984, Brazilians across the country took to the streets, demanding an end to more than twenty years of military dictatorship. Over a million protesters attended one rally in São Paulo. The generals finally gave up power a year later, and a sense of hope emerged that ordinary people could at last choose who should govern Brazil. Today, an elected president and national government run the nation's affairs. Each of the country's twenty-six states has its own elected politicians to make local decisions.

THE LONG ROAD TO FREEDOM

The move toward democracy was slow and difficult. In 1985, the first freely elected government since 1964 had to face an economy in tatters. At the same time, people's expectations were high. They wanted immediate improvements in wages and an end to skyrocketing prices. The first civilian president, Tancredo Neves, died within two months of taking office, and it took another three years for the government to pass a new constitution for Brazilian citizens. The 1988 constitution guaranteed the right to free speech and the right to strike. It outlawed the use of torture, which had been widespread under the military regime. It also gave sixteen-year-olds the right to vote for the first time.

▼ The National Congress in Brasília, with its twin towers and bowl-like structures, is the place where politicians gather to debate and vote on policies that shape Brazil's future. The futuristic architecture symbolizes a changing, modern face to the country.

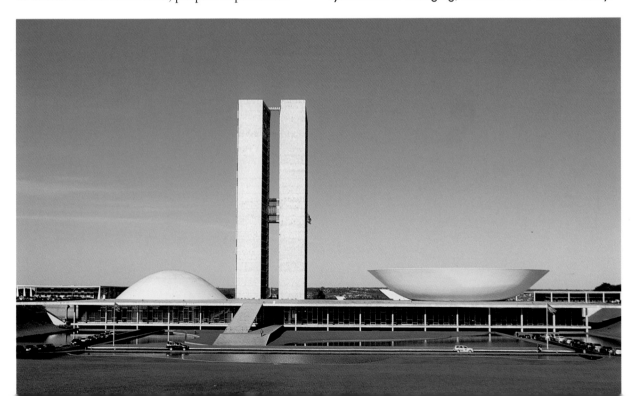

More than eighty million Brazilians voted in the 1989 election, but confidence in democratic government soon faded. People did not notice a marked improvement in their lives, and many still did not trust politicians. For them, politics was a corrupt business that kept money and power in the hands of a few. A corruption scandal at the highest level of government did not help. In 1992, President Fernando Collor de Mello was thrown out of office when he was accused of illegally pocketing millions of dollars. Although the Brazilian Supreme Court later acquitted him of the corruption charges, Collor de Mello was not allowed to stand for public office again.

THE PEOPLE'S GOVERNMENT

After two unsuccessful attempts, Luis Inácio Lula da Silva, known as "Lula," finally became president at the end of 2002. Lula brought great hope to poor Brazilians. From a poor background himself, Lula was once a metalworker in a car factory who became a popular trade union leader in São Paulo's industrial heartland. Since taking office, Lula has made it a government priority to fight corruption and to take active steps to fight poverty in Brazil. Although progress has been slower than some supporters had hoped, Lula's government has begun a nationwide program, called "Zero Hunger," to help the 46 million Brazilians who live on less than a dollar a day.

 Did You Know?

In the 2002 election, President Luis Inácio Lula da Silva won the largest share of the vote in Brazil's history.

Focus on: Gilberto Gil

Brazil's Minister of Culture comes from a different background than most politicians. Since the 1960s, Gilberto Gil has been one of the most famous singer-songwriters in Brazil. As a pop star, Gilberto outraged the military government with lyrics that criticized their regime. He spent time in prison and had to flee to the United Kingdom for two years. At the ceremony to celebrate Lula's election victory, Gilberto wore clothes that reflected his African roots and sang songs of celebration. As a minister, Gilberto wants to bring culture and hope to landless Brazilians, and to those who live in the poor neighborhoods of Brazil's cities.

▶ Despite his responsibilities as a government minister, Gilberto Gil still performs concerts for his adoring fans.

PRESSURE GROUPS

As an alternative to mainstream politics, many Brazilians join pressure groups to voice their views and needs. The Landless Workers Movement (MST) campaigns for fairer distribution of land in Brazil. The MST began in 1984 in Rio Grande do Sul, but today it has 100,000 supporters in every corner of the country. Under Brazil's constitution, people have no right to leave land unused when landless Brazilians are dying from hunger. Half a million large farms occupy three-quarters of Brazil's cropland, including 370 million acres (150 million hectares) that are left under-used. Meanwhile, more than six million families struggle to make a living on the remainder. Another four million families have no land at all. Distribution of land has historically been unequal in Brazil, but despite attempts to share out land more fairly, little change has been made. Some people argue that government backing for large farms that grow crops such as soy beans for export and a lack of support for farmers growing food for local markets have made the situation worse.

Amerindian tribes also club together to make their voices heard. Every year, on April 19, Amerindians from all over the country gather in

Focus on: Land Grabs

The MST organizes invasions of unused land. Working together, MST members set up camp, building communal kitchens, toilets, and even schools for their children. They train each other in better farming techniques and in the basics of reading and writing. Landowners who lose their land can claim compensation from the government. Nevertheless, these land occupations have led to fierce battles between MST members, landowners, and police, and MST families risk being evicted.

▼ Members of the MST set up camp illegally on the side of a highway near Illheus in the northeast. Just thirty families own most of the huge area of land in the northeast.

Brasília for the "Day of the Indian." Successive Brazilian governments have pledged to protect Amerindian livelihoods and communal ownership of their land, but they have not matched their words with actions. Amerindians gather to protest these broken promises.

WOMEN'S RIGHTS

Women are perhaps the biggest pressure group of all. Under Brazil's 1988 constitution, women were given the same legal rights as men. Yet many women still earn less in the workplace than men, and few women hold positions of power. Many women's rights groups in Brazil are working to change this situation. In the northeast, the Rural Women Workers' Movement campaigns for fairer wages for women farmers. Other groups support women who have been victims of sexual harassment and violence.

 Did You Know?

Since 1970, the percentage of the economically active population represented by women has risen to more that 40 percent. This balance is not reflected in Brazil's government, however, where women hold fewer than 7 percent of the seats in parliament.

Focus on: Marina Silva

Marina Silva is one of the very few women to hold a powerful position in Brazil's government. She grew up in a rubber-tapping community in Acre state. When she was sixteen years old, she moved to Rio Branco, the state capital, where she learned to read and write. Later, she founded the rubber-tappers' union with Chico Mendes to fight for better conditions for the rubber tappers. After Chico's murder in 1988, she moved into politics on a bigger scale. In 1994, she was elected as a senator of Acre state, and today she is Brazil's Minister for the Environment. Her job is one of the biggest in government because she makes decisions about how to use the country's vast natural resources.

▼ Unlike many of her predecessors, Marina Silva makes a point of sharing ideas with ordinary people to find solutions to the country's environmental problems.

CHAPTER 6

Energy and Resources

As the country's economy has grown, Brazilians have become the biggest consumers of energy in South America. Brazil is the tenth largest energy consumer in the world. Oil is by far the most important energy source. Since the 1970s, oil has been pumped from deepwater fields off the coast to provide half the country's needs. Sophisticated technology is helping to discover new oil reserves, particularly in the offshore Campos Basin north of Rio de Janeiro. With expanding offshore fields, Brazil is now the third largest oil producer in South America, but it still consumes far more oil than it produces, and imports half its oil requirements.

ALTERNATIVE ENERGY

Discoveries of natural gas in the Amazon basin and a new network of gas pipelines may increase the importance of natural gas in the future. Since 1999, Brazil has received natural gas from neighboring Bolivia through a

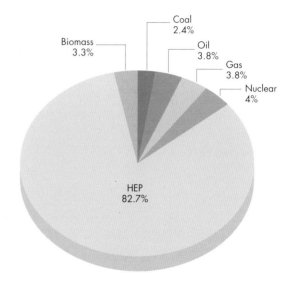

▲ Electricity production by type

Biomass 3.3%
Coal 2.4%
Oil 3.8%
Gas 3.8%
Nuclear 4%
HEP 82.7%

2,000-mile (3,150-km) pipeline known as Gasbol. In return, the Brazilian government agreed to build new natural gas plants in Bolivia. Nevertheless, natural gas provided only 5.7 percent of the country's energy mix in 2002. Brazil's oil and gas supplies will not last forever, and burning these fossil fuels pollutes the atmosphere. Hydroelectric power (HEP) is a cleaner and more sustainable source of energy that uses dams to harness the power of running water. Brazil has many fast-flowing rivers to generate HEP, and more than 80 percent of Brazil's electricity now comes from this source. Itaipú in Paraná state is the largest dam in the world. Built jointly by Brazil and Paraguay, the dam is 5 miles (8 km) long, and produces enough electricity to power the whole of southern Brazil.

◄ A new pipeline is laid near Corumba in the west of Brazil. Once complete, the pipeline will transport natural gas from Bolivia all the way to São Paulo.

▲ Completed in 2002, the Cana Brava dam in the eastern Amazon basin is the first of twenty-seven new dams. Its construction caused widespread protest because it will flood 4,630 square miles (12,000 sq km) of rain forest and threaten 75,000 people.

DAM-BUILDING

Other large dams have been built to tap the energy of the Amazon's tributaries, but many Brazilians are angered by dam building. Thousands of people were forced to move after the construction of the Tucuruí dam on the Tocantins River because the dam created a reservoir that flooded 1,100 square miles (2,850 sq km) of land. Many of the displaced people were not compensated. Another problem is that trees were not cleared before the reservoir flooded the land. Gradually, the rotting vegetation has made the reservoir water too toxic for fish and has created an enormous breeding ground for malarial mosquitoes.

Did You Know?

More than one million people in Brazil have been forced to move from their homes because dam-building caused reservoirs to flood their land. About 13,124 square miles (34,000 sq km) have been flooded—an area larger than Belgium.

Energy Data

- Energy consumption as % of world total: 2.3%
- Energy consumption by sector (% of total), 1999:
  Industry: 47
  Transportation: 30
  Agriculture: 5
  Services: 5
  Residential: 13
- CO_2 emissions as % of world total: 1.3
- CO_2 emissions per capita in tons per year: 1.8

Source: World Resources Institute

Focus on: Alcohol-burning Cars

Brazilians have developed a substitute for oil to fuel the country's vehicles. Since the 1970s, Brazilians have driven cars that run on pure alcohol (ethanol) made from sugar cane. Ethanol-fueled cars release less pollution and reduce the country's oil bills. In the 1980s, 75 percent of new cars in Brazil ran on ethanol. By the end of the 1990s, however, the ethanol-powered car had almost disappeared from Brazil's streets. As oil prices fell, it became cheaper to run a car on gasoline. Since 2002, the government has backed an ethanol revival, and, as oil prices rise, this fuel is becoming more competitive again. Better vehicle designs and lower taxes on ethanol-fueled vehicles may also help boost the number of these cleaner cars on Brazil's roads.

 This gigantic machine at the Rio Dolce iron ore mine, part of the Greater Carajás Development Program, is used to scoop up iron ore. The ore is then transported along a conveyor to the refinery.

MINERAL RICHES

Brazil has vast quantities of natural resources, both above and below the ground. Most of the gold discovered in the 1700s was found in the mud washed down by rivers in Minas Gerais state. No one knows exactly who discovered this precious metal, but news of the discovery of gold spread fast. Brazilians and Portuguese *bandeirantes* flocked to Minas Gerais to seek their fortune. Sugarcane farmers gave up their plantations nearer the coast and brought their slaves with them to dig for gold. In the 1720s, diamonds were discovered as well, and many people became incredibly rich. Although the region is still a source of many precious gemstones, the glory days of the gold rush ended in the 1800s.

With improved road and air transportation, new deposits of minerals have been uncovered in remote parts of the Amazon basin. In 1967, a helicopter pilot flew over Carajás, eastern Amazonia, and saw a clearing of red rock amid the green carpet of rain forest. It turned out to be the biggest deposit of iron ore in the world. Today, the twenty-five smelting furnaces of the Greater Carajás Development Program heat the ore to turn it into pig iron near the gigantic iron ore mine. Some of the iron ore is taken on the 560-mile- (900-km-) long railroad that connects the mine to São Luis on the coast, to be shipped abroad.

? Did You Know?

The mines, furnaces, and other developments of the Greater Carajás Development Program cover an area bigger than Texas and California combined.

RAIN FOREST TIMBER

Timber is another important resource from the Amazon. Most of the timber is bought by businesses in southern Brazil to make furniture or to supply construction yards with plywood. Rain forest hardwoods such as mahogany are renowned for their superior quality and bring high prices on the international market. For every mahogany tree harvested, however, as much as 3,000 square feet (280 square meters) of forest is destroyed. Some loggers take mahogany trees illegally from protected land.

RUBBER BOOM AND BUST

The rubber industry exploits one Amazon forest resource without depleting the forest. Originally used by the Amerindians, rubber comes from a sticky liquid called latex found under the bark of the rubber tree. In the 1800s, the city of Manaus became the center of a rubber boom, thanks to the invention of rubber tires. Although 20,000 rubber tappers still work in Acre state, rubber is no longer a prized commodity because many other countries now produce it.

At Xapuri, in Acre state, rubber tappers are enjoying a new boom in business. To fight the spread of HIV and AIDS, Brazilians need increasing numbers of condoms. The latex factory in Xapuri no longer makes tires but instead produces more than 100 million condoms a year. Profits from manufacturing condoms are creating thousands of jobs, and will help to safeguard the future of the environment and the health of the nation.

▼ Despite the damage to the environment, logging tropical timber is an important economic activity in the Amazon region.

CHAPTER 7

Economy and Income

Fifty years ago, most of Brazil's exports were farm products such as coffee and sugar cane. Pernambuco state in the northeast once produced the entire world supply of sugar. It is still a major sugar-producing region. Brazil remains the world's largest coffee producer, and 300,000 farmers rely on coffee growing for their livelihoods. Cattle ranching is also important, and Brazil now exports 590,000 tons (600,000 tonnes) of beef every year. Brazil's modern economy, however, is even more diversified. Nowadays, Brazilians also work in factories making steel, petrochemicals, and cars. Millions of others work in service industries, such as tourism, banking, and retail.

MADE IN BRAZIL

In 1968, Brazil's military government embarked on a plan to turn Brazil from a farmyard into an industrial powerhouse. The government promised overseas companies low taxes and a share of the growing markets of South America. It encouraged these companies to open factories in Brazil. This way, more goods could be made in Brazil itself, and people would need fewer expensive imports.

RISING DEBTS

To jump-start this industrial growth, the government borrowed millions of dollars to build a modern network of roads, dams, pipelines, power stations, and factory sites. At the time, interest rates were low, and overseas banks were keen to lend the money. In the early 1980s, the industrialized economies went into recession, and governments raised interest rates—including rates on loans to countries such as Brazil. These higher interest rates

▼ Using modern farming techniques and better grass varieties, today's Brazilian cattle ranchers are enjoying a boom in business.

meant that Brazil could not even pay back the interest, let alone the debt itself. At the same time, Brazil could not sell many exports to the industrialized world. Brazil's debt soared out of control, and to keep the economy afloat, the government sold off many state-owned companies and cut spending on basic services such as health and education.

In 2005, Brazil was still massively in debt, but its economy was making enough money to keep its lenders happy. For many overseas companies, Brazil is an attractive place to set up an operation. In Brasília, hi-tech companies such as IBM, Apple, Intel, and Microsoft have bases in the shiny new office blocks in the Vale do Silicio, Brazil's own silicon valley. Local hi-tech companies in IT and biotechnology are doing well, too, and the Brazilian company Embraer is now the fourth biggest aircraft manufacturer in the world.

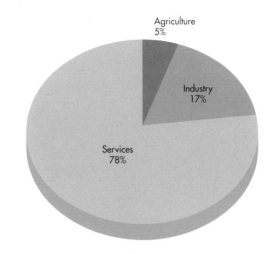

▲ Economy by sector

 Did You Know?

Of the ten biggest companies in Brazil today, four of them are American—General Motors, Ford, Texaco, and Exxon-Mobil.

Focus on: The Valley of Death

São Paulo state is the economic engine that drives the Brazilian economy. About two-thirds of Brazil's industries are concentrated in this state, in places such as Cubatão valley, the heart of Brazil's petrochemical industry. In the 1970s, Cubatão was nicknamed "the valley of death," because its poisonous industrial waste and filthy air made it one of the most polluted places on earth. People living in the valley suffered many health problems. Birth defects among children were commonplace. Some children were even born without brains. For adults living in the valley, the chances of developing lung, throat, and mouth cancer were twice as high as in other areas. Since 1983, Cubatão has been cleaned up. Big polluters now receive

heavy fines, and factories are closed down if pollution levels reach dangerous limits.

▼ Cubatão's chimneys still belch poisonous fumes into the atmosphere twenty-four hours a day.

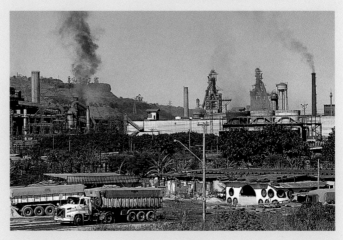

Economic Data

- Gross National Income (GNI) in U.S.$: 552,096,000,000
- World rank by GNI: 13
- GNI per capita in U.S.$: 3,090
- World rank by GNI per capita: 96
- Economic growth: 4.2%

Source: World Bank

RICH WORLD, POOR WORLD

Brazil may have the ninth largest economy in the world, but its riches are far from evenly shared. The richest 10 percent of the population receives about 50 percent of the country's income, while the poorest 50 percent receives just 10 percent. About one-third of all Brazilians live on less than U.S.$1 a day, and the gap between the richest and poorest is wider than almost anywhere else in the world, both in rural areas and in the cities.

NEW OPPORTUNITIES

The northeast is especially poor. Income per capita is half the national average, and more than half the population of this region cannot read or write. Much of the best farmland is owned by a few, while millions of others have no land at all. Instead, people move from place to place in search of work. New projects, however, are allowing people to help themselves. One example is a simple and cheap project to save water. In a region where few people have access to fresh water, farmers are digging small dams to capture precious rainwater and channel it into their fields. These irrigation schemes are helping to turn parched farmland into lush, productive fields of fruit, vegetables, and cereals. Regular water supplies are also creating

▼ This market street in the small town of Barreirinhas is typical of many of the towns in Brazil's poorest state, Maranhão, in northeast Brazil. Life in the northeast is a world away from the modern cities of Brazil's rich southeast region.

new opportunities in wine-making. Vineyards around cities such as Recife now produce 880,000 gallons (4 million liters) of wine a year and employ more than 30,000 people.

CHILDREN IN POVERTY

Some people have no home at all. Street children have to make a living and fend for themselves. Many are at great risk of catching sexually transmitted diseases because they are forced into prostitution to make money. Others have joined drug gangs, acting as messengers for drug dealers and users. Blaming these children for the rise in crime, vigilantes have formed death squads that murder street children to remove them from the city's streets. Child-care agencies estimate that between two and six street children are murdered in Rio every day. Yet, according to Amnesty International, 90 percent of these murders go unpunished. A number of organizations are now giving street children a chance of a better life. Shelters are springing up where children can get away from the dangers of the streets, learn new skills, and go to school.

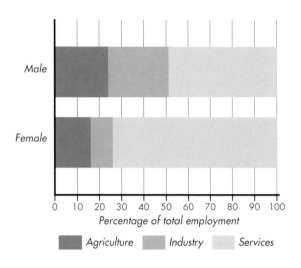

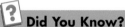

▲ Labor force by sector and gender

? Did You Know?

One percent of the country's landowners control more than half the land in Brazil.

▼ Street children sort through rubbish in Salvador. Brazil's city streets are home to about ten million children, some as young as five years old.

CHAPTER 8

Global Connections

Goods made in Brazil are exported all over the world. About half of Brazil's exports are sold in the United States and the European Union, but Brazil is also creating new trading partnerships closer to home. To boost trade with its neighbors, Brazil is an important member of Mercosur, an alliance of South American countries. Mercosur has set up a "free-trade zone" so that companies in Brazil, Argentina, Paraguay, Peru, and Uruguay can buy goods from and sell goods to each other without paying extra taxes. This way companies can make goods more cheaply, and prices fall in the shops, too.

NEW DEALS AND FRIENDSHIPS

Brazil is building new friendships with individual countries in other parts of the world. Notably, the government is strengthening ties

▼ Harvests from the vast fields of soy beans in Brazil are now exported to China and countries in Europe.

with China, Brazil's third biggest trading partner and today's fastest growing economy. The trade works both ways. Already, Brazilians build passenger jets in northeast China, while the Chinese have helped to launch Brazilian satellites into orbit. To ease China's growing need for energy and food, Brazil is providing China with sugarcane and ethanol, and Brazilian farmers are planting more soy beans in the Amazon region to help feed the millions that now live in Chinese cities. In return, there are plans to use Chinese technology to rebuild parts of Brazil's crumbling road and rail networks. With so much cooperation between the two countries, some people believe that China will soon become Brazil's biggest trading partner.

Brazil has also joined forces with South Africa and India. In 2003, leaders of the three countries met in Brasília to sign an agreement to promote greater cooperation. Collectively known as the "G-3," these three powerful developing countries are fighting together for a fairer share of world trade for poor nations. They want rich countries to remove trade barriers, such as taxes on imports, that make it impossible for poorer

countries to compete. In particular, farmers in poorer countries struggle because, while rich countries subsidise agriculture to make domestic products cheaper, imported goods from farms elsewhere are taxed. The G-3 countries believe that this is unfair and that it must be changed.

Focus on: Car Culture

Today, Brazil offers incentives such as low taxes to foreign companies to attract business to the country. German car-maker, Volkswagen (VW) has operated in Brazil for more than fifty years. VW employs 26,000 Brazilians in its five factories. As a young man, President Lula worked in VW's factory in São Bernardo do Campo, São Paulo state, where he made a name for himself as a trade union leader. In 2002, the São Bernardo plant was modernized to make the latest VW Polo model. Local companies benefit as they make components for Volkswagen cars. At the same time, VW can take advantage of the growing market for cars in South America. This way, the company can expand its customer base and make more profit in the process.

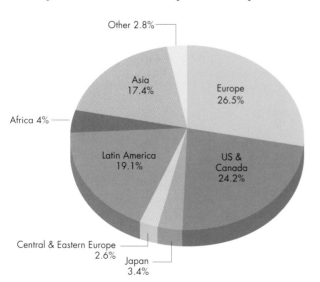

▲ Destination of exports by major trading region

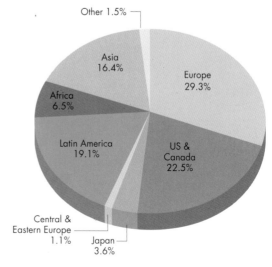

▲ Origin of imports by major trading region

HOSTS TO THE WORLD

With such a large economy, Brazil now has a powerful voice on the world stage. In 1992, Brazil hosted the world's first Earth Summit. World leaders and advisers gathered in Rio de Janeiro to put together a global action plan for the twenty-first century known as Agenda 2. This plan put protection of the environment as a top priority. Although many of the promises made in Rio have not been kept, this summit was an important moment in history because it drew attention to the destruction to the world's environments and resources.

Every other year in the southern city of Porto Alegre, Brazil plays host to the World Social Forum. This gathering of activists is an alternative summit to the World Economic Forum, a meeting of the leaders of the developed countries that takes place in Switzerland. More than 100,000 people came to the World Social Forum in January 2005, including the presidents of Brazil and Venezuela. Over six days, thousands of meetings took place. Together, small interest groups from all over the world discussed alternative ways of fighting poverty and of making a fairer, cleaner and healthier world for all. The discussions may be serious, but the atmosphere at the World Social Forum is bright, colorful, and loud.

▼ A great mix of interest groups gather at the World Social Forum in Porto Alegre.

▲ With guaranteed press attention wherever he goes, Ronaldo is able to raise awareness of the problems faced by the billions of people who live in poverty.

PLAYING SOCCER AND FIGHTING POVERTY

For decades, people around the world have been in awe of the skill of Brazil's soccer players. Ronaldo, one of the country's top soccer stars, is now using his fame to bring attention to the problems of the world's poor. Although he plays for Real Madrid in Spain, one of the world's richest soccer clubs, Ronaldo has not forgotten the poverty of his childhood in Bento Ribeiro, a suburb on the edge of Rio de Janeiro. Off the soccer field, Ronaldo works for the United Nations (UN) as a goodwill ambassador. Drawing big crowds wherever he goes, Ronaldo highlights the problems of poverty, raising money for UN projects to help poor children in Brazil and to raise awareness about HIV/AIDS.

A TASTE OF BRAZIL

The rhythms of Brazil can be heard everywhere. In the United Kingdom alone, more than a hundred *samba* schools teach people to play drums and practice their dance steps. Brazilian food and drink is catching on as well. Bars selling *guaraná*—a natural energizer made from a forest fruit found in the Amazon—are appearing in many cities. And *caipirinha*, made from sugarcane-based alcohol, crushed limes, and ice, is the cocktail of choice at bars in cities such as London, New York, and Madrid.

CHAPTER 9

Transportation and Communications

Brazilians need a complicated transportation system to link different parts of their vast country. Most Brazilians travel by road, despite the distances involved. Buses are cheap and comfortable even though journeys between some cities can take days. Rich Brazilians save time by flying. With the capital city, Brasília, as its central hub, the country has a network of nearly 4,000 airports serving every part of the country. However, since 2001, a new, cheap airline called Gol has made it possible for ordinary Brazilians to fly for the first time. Transporting passengers to forty different destinations in Brazil, Gol has already captured a quarter of Brazil's market in air travel. The airline is now expanding into international markets. Gol started flights to Argentina in 2004, and plans to add routes to Uruguay, Paraguay and Bolivia.

NEW FRONTIERS IN THE JUNGLE

In the 1970s, the military government put together an ambitious plan to improve access to remoter parts of the Amazon basin. The 1,864-mile- (3,000-km) long Trans-Amazonian highway was built in 1970, and new settlers followed in the tracks of the bulldozers. In 1975, the BR364 road connected the Amazonian states of Rondônia and Acre with the south, and work has begun on a new highway that will connect one side of Amazonia to the other in the north. Smaller roads branch out from the main roads to create a whole network. During the rainy season, however, many of these smaller roads turn into rivers of mud.

With its gentle gradient and wide channels, the Amazon River provides a transportation route for goods and people. Large boats can sail up and down the river and its tributaries, thousands of miles inland. The Amazon has two major ports, Belém at its mouth and Manaus further upstream. Some of the old steamers that used to transport rubber have been converted into cruise ships for luxury tours along the river.

▲ Many parts of the Amazon region are still only accessible by boat.

MANAGING THE TRAFFIC

As urbanization increases and more Brazilians own cars, many cities are frequently clogged with traffic. With three million vehicles on the road on weekdays, São Paulo's city authorities struggle to keep the traffic moving. Here, traffic jams are longer than in any city in the developed world and residents spend an average of nearly three hours traveling between home and work.

The people of Curitiba have learned from the problems of other cities and, since 1965, have planned carefully to keep the traffic moving in their city. Although the city is ten times bigger than it was fifty years ago, people in Curitiba can travel easily and cheaply. Two thousand buses each carry 300 passengers along special bus lanes that crisscross the city, and there are 93 miles (150 km) of bicycle lanes. Because it is easier to travel by bus or bicycle, there are now 30 percent fewer cars on the roads than thirty years ago, when the population was half what it is today. Travel times in the city are nearly twice as fast as in São Paulo. Cities across the world are using Curitiba as an example of how to manage traffic successfully.

 Did You Know?

Car ownership in São Paulo has tripled in thirty years, and during rush hour traffic jams can stretch for 62 miles (100 km) through the city.

Transportation and Communications Data

- Total roads: 1,071,181 miles/1,724,929 km
- Total paved roads: 58,915 miles/94,871 km
- Total unpaved roads: 1,012,266 miles/ 1,630,058 km
- Total railways: 18,276 miles/29,412 km
- Major airports: 698
- Cars per 1,000 people: 120
- Mobile phones per 1,000 people: 264
- Personal computers per 1,000 people: 75
- Internet users per 1,000 people: 82

Source: World Bank and CIA World Factbook

▼ Curitiba's modern bus terminals enable people to get on and off buses quickly and easily.

CALLING LONG DISTANCE

Before the 1970s, it was very difficult to communicate over long distances in Brazil, let alone speak to someone overseas. The military government, however, spent a lot of money to build a telecommunications network across the country in the 1970s. Today, it is easy to call people in most parts of Brazil. Cell phones are now commonplace, and in 2005 the Global System for Mobile Communications (GSM) became the country's leading cellular technology.

Brazil has dozens of daily newspapers and several weekly news magazines. With high levels of illiteracy, however, television and radio are important ways to keep many people informed. Nearly every Brazilian home has a radio, and most have TVs, too. Family-owned TV companies have grown from small businesses into enormous corporations. Based in Rio, the Globo TV company is the biggest. Globo makes dramas, reality TV shows, and soap operas (or "telenovelas") that are exported to Africa, Europe, China, and other countries in South America.

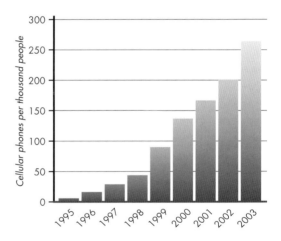

▲ Cellular phone use, 1995-2003

 Did You Know?

More than 47 million Brazilians owned a cell phone by 2003, nearly a tenfold increase since 1997. Brazil has 280 internet service providers, the largest number in South America.

◀ By using satellite communications instead of cables and pylons on land, wireless technology enables Brazilians to communicate easily with other parts of the country or abroad, no matter where they live.

THE PLUGGED AND THE UNPLUGGED

Today, the Internet is changing the way in which many Brazilians work and communicate. Using the Internet, companies can do business with the rest of the world, and people can keep in touch across huge distances. Cybercafes that give free or very cheap internet access are sprouting up in Brazil's cities. The cybercafe in Cidade Tiradentes, one of the poorest areas of São Paulo, offers a possible passport out of poverty. Here, people can search for jobs more easily, and email their applications to anywhere in the country. At the same time, they can teach themselves computer skills to improve their chances of getting a better job.

In rural areas it is often too expensive to set up communication networks. Many villages have no telephone lines, and most people have never touched a computer. Soon even the remotest parts of Brazil will no longer be unplugged. In August 2004, a French-built satellite called Amazonas was launched from Russia. Amazonas will provide the opportunity for the latest telecommunication services, including broadband Internet, to every corner of the country.

Focus on: Soap Scandal

Soap opera actors are big celebrities in Brazil, and in 1992, the whole country was gripped by the news of a tragedy involving two of its most famous soap stars. The actress Daniela Perez was brutally murdered, stabbed eighteen times with a pair of scissors. Her co-star, Guilherme de Padua, was charged with her murder and sentenced to nineteen years in prison.

▼ Satellite broadcasting means that TV is available in almost every part of Brazil. Here, family members watch TV in their house near Rio Branco, within the Amazon rain forest.

CHAPTER 10

Education and Health

For most Brazilians, a good education is very important. With qualifications and skills learned at school, they have a better chance of making a decent living as adults. Parents place high value on education for their children, and the availability of schools is an important priority in deciding where to live. As in other areas of Brazilian life, however, education is marked by a wide gap between the rich and poor.

? Did You Know??

Fourteen million Brazilians have never been to school. Of all the Brazilians with college degrees, 80 percent are white, and only 2 percent are black.

STRUGGLING SCHOOLS

School is compulsory for all Brazil's 30 million children between the ages of seven and fourteen. If they can afford it, many families send their children to private schools where the facilities match any good school in the world. Public education is free to all Brazilians, but many of these schools lack resources and equipment. Teachers' pay in public schools is very low, too, and some schools struggle to find enough qualified teachers. Inequalities continue

▼ In Recife and a number of other cities in the northeast, a charity called PLAN provides mobile libraries to give children a better chance of learning to read.

into higher education. Even though any student who passes the tough entrance exams can go to a public university for free, the students that attended private school are usually the ones who make the grade.

▲ Private schools boast the latest technology to help students achieve the highest grades.

A RIGHT TO EDUCATION

The 1988 constitution that marked the rebirth of democratic Brazil recognized the right to free education for both young people and adults. The reality, however, is that many Brazilian children do not go to school at all. In the northeast, nearly one-third of the children did not even complete fifth grade. Each school year, parents have to buy uniforms, school supplies, and books for their children—items that many cannot afford. Others do not have the money for the bus fare to school. Instead, more than three million children start work at ten years old to earn money to support the rest of the family. Where schools lie in territory controlled by drug gangs in city *favelas*, some children are too scared to go to school. More than 12 percent of Brazilians reach adulthood without knowing how to read or write, one of the highest rates of illiteracy in South America.

To ensure that the right to education becomes a reality, President Lula's government wants to guarantee a school place for every child. It plans to eradicate illiteracy altogether. Subsidies for school transportation and meals will help to ease the financial burden on poorer families. The government is also investing in literacy programs for adults, focusing on poorer regions such as the northeast.

HEALTH FOR ALL

Although Brazil has many hospitals, clinics, and doctors, the health of Brazil's poor is a cause for concern, particularly in rural areas. Most of the health services are concentrated in the cities, and without a regular supply of safe water, villagers are at high risk of catching treatable diseases such as diarrhea. Basic health problems affect the poorer residents of Brazilian cities, too. Hunger and malnutrition are common because many poorer Brazilians do not eat a balanced diet.

The 1988 constitution granted all Brazilians the right to health care. To put this into practice, the government set up the Family Health Program in 1994, dispatching teams of doctors

▲ In poorer districts of Recife doctors have to make the most of a limited range of medicines and equipment to treat their patients.

and nurses to tackle health problems in local communities. Each team is responsible for 3,000 people and provides medicines as well as advice on how to ward off disease and stay healthy. The teams also train community members to provide basic treatment themselves.

MOSQUITO MENACE

Malaria is a problem in the Amazon, with 99 percent of Brazil's malaria cases occurring in this region. Carried by *anopheles* mosquitoes, malaria can be deadly. Many missionaries died

Focus on: Leprosy

With about 40,000 new cases each year, Brazil has one of the world's highest rates of leprosy. Many Brazilians fear leprosy because the advanced stages of the disease leave victims severely disfigured and disabled. In Brazil, thirty-three "hospital colonies"

isolate sufferers from the rest of society, often in poor conditions. Nevertheless, leprosy is curable, and the health ministry is investing in better treatment and support for leprosy patients so that they can return to normal lives.

of malaria during the years under Portuguese rule, and today Amerindian communities are still struck by the disease. Development projects such as road construction and mining opened up new frontiers in the Amazon in the early 1970s. Because some of the road builders and miners carried the malaria parasite, they brought the disease into the rain forest with them. Mosquitoes soon passed it along. Today, there is some success in fighting malaria by identifying the symptoms early and giving people treatment before the disease takes hold. It is a never-ending battle. Even when drugs to combat malaria are available, mosquitoes are becoming immune to their effects and new, stronger drugs have to be developed.

Another disease carried by mosquitoes is dengue. Dengue is sometimes known as "break bone fever" because sufferers experience deep, painful itching inside the bones and a high fever. Although the disease is rarely lethal, it is difficult to treat and people may have to take months off work or school to recover from it. More than half of the dengue cases in Brazil occur in Rio de Janeiro. Standing pools of water in courtyards and streets after heavy rain provide perfect breeding grounds for dengue-carrying mosquitoes.

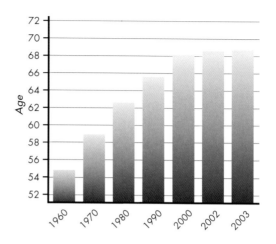

▲ Life expectancy at birth 1960-2003

Education and Health

- Life expectancy at birth, male: 64.9
- Life expectancy at birth, female: 72.8
- Infant mortality rate per 1,000: 30
- Under five mortality rate per 1,000: 36
- Physicians per 1,000 people: 2.1
- Health expenditure as % of GDP: 7.9%
- Education expenditure as % of GDP: 4.7%
- Primary net enrollment: 97%
- Pupil-teacher ratio, primary: 23.0
- Adult literacy as % age 15+: 87.3

Source: United Nations Agencies and World Bank

Focus on: Setting an Example to the World

Perhaps the greatest health threat to Brazilians today is from HIV/AIDS. Brazil has become a model for the rest of the world, however, in tackling the disease and in helping those living with HIV/AIDS. The first reported case of AIDS in Brazil was in 1980. By 2003, there were 310,000 cases, mostly in the southeast. Thanks to a widespread education program, however, Brazilians are more aware of how to avoid infection. In spite of the large numbers of Catholics in the population, use of condoms is widespread, and drugs that help those living with HIV are virtually free. These drugs are copies of medicines developed by international pharmaceutical companies but are made locally by Brazilian companies and sold much more cheaply than on the international market. AIDS-related deaths have fallen by 60 percent, and the number of new HIV cases is falling, too.

CHAPTER 11

Culture and Religion

During colonial times, the Portuguese insisted that Catholicism was the only acceptable religion. European missionaries worked hard to spread their message deep into the interior of the country, building churches and schools to convert local people. Although Brazilians today can practice any religion they like, most of them are Catholics.

EVANGELICAL EXPLOSION

Evangelical Protestants are the fastest growing religious group in Brazil. In 1990, followers represented 9 percent of the population, but by 2000 this figure had risen to 15 percent. Nearly half are members of the Assembly of God, the largest evangelical church in Brazil. Another group called the Universal Church of God's Kingdom owns Brazil's third largest TV network. Many young people from poor backgrounds have joined evangelical groups, seeking answers to their economic and personal problems. Followers lead a very strict lifestyle and go to church regularly. Worship services are lively events, full of singing and chanting. In some services, followers speak in tongues, and priests perform faith-healing ceremonies.

Did You Know?

Seventy-two percent of Brazilians are Catholic, but the number of Catholics has fallen in recent years because many have joined the Evangelical Protestant movement. The evangelical church, the Assembly of God, now has at least 13 million followers.

Focus on: Our Lady of Aperecida

Many Brazilian Catholics believe that a terracotta statue of a black female figure in the town of Aperecida, near São Paulo, represents the Virgin Mary. Discovered in 1717, the statue is kept in a special shrine. Next to the shrine, a room is crammed full of gifts from people who have come to give thanks for the miracles they believe the Virgin Mary has granted. In 2002, the soccer player Ronaldo paid a visit to give thanks after Brazil's victory in the World Cup Final.

▲ A family visits the impressive Cathedral da Se in the heart of São Luis, a place of worship for Catholics since it was built in 1629.

WORSHIPPING THE SPIRITS

Amerindian groups were practicing their own faiths long before the Portuguese brought Christianity to Brazil. Many Amerindians still have animist beliefs, worshipping spirits that represent different parts of the environment around them. The Tupi have their own god of love and gods of the sun, the moon, thunder, and lightning. Other Tupi spirits guard animals and birds or protect men when they are hunting. Amerindian priests, or shamans, call on these spirits by making magic potions from forest plants. They believe they can cure people from diseases or act as fortune-tellers.

Millions of Brazilians mix different beliefs to create new religions. In Bahia state, Candomblé plays an important part in many people's lives. This religion combines African slave rituals with Catholicism and Amerindian customs. According to Candomblé, all people have one or two spirits, known as *orixás*, that influence their personalities and guide them through life. Only a Candomblé priest can tell which *orixá* is important, and many people will make offerings to their *orixás* to keep them happy. During a Candomblé ceremony, people use the Yoruba language from West Africa. Food is passed around, and dancing can last throughout the night. Devotees may fall into a trance during which, they believe, they are possessed by their *orixás* who will offer them advice and tell them about their futures.

▶ On the streets of Salvador, the high priestesses of Candomblé are recognizable from their spectacular bustled dresses.

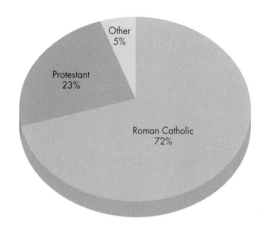

▲ Brazil's major religions

SOUL FOOD

Some of the country's food, music, and dance has links with Africa. On the streets of Salvador, *acarajés* are on sale. These delicious dumplings are made from a mixture of kidney beans, dried prawns, and hot peppers. They are fried in palm oil, an ingredient from West Africa. African slaves were the first to cook a stew called *feijoada*, Brazil's national dish. To add flavor to their food, the slaves collected scraps of pork thrown out by their owners. Modern day *feijoada* is the Brazilian version of African American "soul food." It is a tasty dish made of black beans, pork spareribs and sausages, and salted beef, served with fried onion, toasted manioc, and rice.

Slaves also performed Capoeira, an African martial art. To avoid suspicion from their

▼ Manioc flour is made from the root of cassava, a plant that grows easily in Brazil. As well as a garnish for *feijoada*, Brazilians use manioc flour to thicken stews and to coat pieces of chicken.

masters, slaves disguised Capoeira as a harmless, playful dance. In reality, they practiced Capoeira to defend themselves or even to escape. Capoeira fighters compete against each other with graceful dance moves to try to force their opponents to the ground. A Capoeira fight is accompanied by the plucking sounds of a *berimbau*, a musical instrument that looks like a fishing rod with one string. Although it was banned for many years, Capoeira is making a comeback as many young Brazilians celebrate their African background.

THE "BLACK PEARL"

Sport is another important part of Brazilian culture, and most Brazilians are particularly enthusiastic about soccer. Matches are often like big parties, with colorful flares and flag waving, cheering, and drumming. Nicknamed "the black pearl" by Brazilians, Pelé is possibly the greatest soccer player ever. In 1958, when he was only seventeen, his dazzling skill helped Brazil win

the World Cup for the first time. During his amazing career, Pelé scored more than 1,000 goals. In 1994, Pelé joined the Brazilian government as Minister of Sport for four years. Today, he remains a huge celebrity, both at home and overseas.

DEATH OF A HERO

Many Brazilians have been enthusiastic about Formula One racing since the first Brazilian Grand Prix in 1972. Brazilian Ayrton Senna is one of the all-time greats in the sport. On his fourth birthday, Ayrton sat in the driving seat for the first time—in a go-kart built by his father. As a teenager, he learned to drive through the chaotic traffic of São Paulo, and, by the late 1980s, Ayrton had become a champion racer. He won forty-one Grand Prix races and was crowned world champion three times. Back home, he became a role model for his hard work and honesty. During the 1994 San Marino Grand Prix, however, he was

▲ The graceful slow-motion kicks and acrobatics of Capoeira attract spectators in the streets of Salvador and many other Brazilian cities.

 Did You Know?

Up to 200,000 fans came to watch Pelé's farewell game at the Maracanã stadium in Rio, the world's biggest soccer arena. Brazil's national soccer team is the only one to have qualified for every World Cup Finals tournament, and Brazil is the only country to have won the trophy five times—in 1958, 1962, 1970, 1994, and 2002.

tragically killed in a crash. People across Brazil were devastated by his death, especially because millions saw the crash live on TV. Half a million people followed his coffin through the streets of São Paulo. The Brazilians have not forgotten their hero—a cartoon character, schools, shops, and even highways are named after him.

CHAPTER 12

Leisure and Tourism

For those Brazilians who can afford to take time off work, many are happy to spend their vacations in their own country. After all, Brazil has many different cultures and environments to savor, as well as more than 5,000 miles (8,000 km) of coastline. Inland, the Amazon has its own beaches because sandy material builds up on the riverbanks. To escape city life on the weekends, rich families from São Paulo and Rio de Janeiro own beach apartments or chalets. The beach is an important place for both rich and poor Brazilians, however. No matter what their income, everybody can swim, sunbathe, or play sports on the sand. In the south, where winds blowing across the Atlantic Ocean whip up the waves, surfing is a popular sport.

DANCING TO BRAZILIAN BEATS

Dancing is a favorite pastime for many Brazilians. In the northeast, *forró* is an old type of dance music with Portuguese and African influences that reflect Brazil's past. *Forró* musicians play guitars and drums with an accordion, a flute, and an instrument called a *ganzá*—a little metal box full of pebbles. Further south, the *lambada* is a popular dance. Performing the *lambada* takes a lot of practice—along the promenade of Porto Seguro, the birthplace of the *lambada*, couples show off their sensual moves as they twist and turn at breakneck speed. Young people who live in the poorer neighborhoods of Rio gather at their own kind of parties, known as "funk balls." Baile funk is a type of music that mixes loud, fast electronic rhythms with rap and hip-hop.

▼ Weekend sunbathers crowd on to Ipanema Beach in Rio de Janeiro.

With so much to offer, Brazil is becoming a major destination for vacationers around the world. Today, more international airline routes fly directly to different Brazilian cities than ever before. The increased tourist trade has benefited Brazilians. One million job vacancies have been created in the hotel trade, and thousands of other people are training to be guides, travel agents, and restaurant owners.

NEW ATTRACTIONS

Salvador's airport has become a new international hub, and tourism is now a major source of income for the city and its surroundings. Salvador's interesting mix of cultures, people, and food is a major attraction. The city has 154 beautiful churches, and the buildings and cobbled streets of the central Pelourinho district have been carefully restored. From Salvador, tourists can easily reach some of the country's best beaches to go swimming, fishing, or windsurfing. Meanwhile, hikers head for the mountains, canyons, and waterfalls of Chapada Diamantina national park, a seven-hour bus ride from the city.

 Did You Know?

Rio de Janeiro is Brazil's top tourist destination. Nicknamed *cidade maravilhosa* or "marvellous city" by the Brazilians, 40 percent of the country's international visitors spend time in the city.

▲ The breathtaking views of Rio from the summit of Corcovado mountain are among the many tourist attractions in the city.

Tourism in Brazil

📂 Tourist arrivals, millions: 3.783
📂 Earnings from tourism in U.S.$: 2,672,999,936
📂 Tourism as % foreign earnings: 3.2
📂 Tourist departures, millions: 1.861
📂 Expenditure on tourism in U.S.$: 2,873,999,872

Source: World Bank

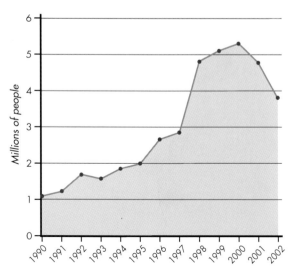

▲ Changes in international tourism, 1990-2002

GOING GREEN

One of the fastest growing areas of the Brazilian tourist market is eco-tourism. Often organized in small groups, eco-tourism packages aim to give visitors a chance to experience natural environments and different cultures without damaging them. At the same time, eco-tourism gives local people a better chance of making a living in areas where there were previously few opportunities. On eco-tourism trips in the Amazon, tourists experience the thrill of fishing for piranha in flooded forests, kayaking through caiman-infested waters, and learning more about the Amerindian way of life by visiting villages and meeting the local people.

Three hours from Brasília, local communities make money from eco-tourism in the Chapada dos Veadeiros national park. One-third of Brazil's plant and animal species are found in the park's tropical grasslands (*cerrado*), and the park contains some spectacular waterfalls. In São Jorge village, local miners are retraining as wildlife experts and guides to lead groups of tourists to different parts of the park. Others in São Jorge make money from selling jam, wild flowers, and souvenirs to their visitors.

▼ Guests at the Ariau Jungle eco-tourist lodge can experience the magnificent rain forest environment right on their doorstep. The lodge is built on stilts on the banks of the Rio Negro, one of the main arteries of the Amazon.

THE ECO-TOURISM BANDWAGON

Despite its advantages, eco-tourism can be a mixed blessing. By giving tourists the chance to see special environments close up, eco-tourism can harm areas that are particularly sensitive to outside interference, such as areas of virgin Amazon rain forest. Elsewhere, the "eco-tourism" name does not match the reality at all. Luxury hotels are sometimes built under the name of eco-tourism even though they lead to the destruction of valuable environments and put great pressure on resources such as energy and water.

 Did You Know?

Each year, about one million eco-tourists visit Brazil. While Brazil's tourism sector is growing by 3 percent a year overall, eco-tourism is up by 15 percent.

Focus on: Carnival: The Greatest Show on Earth

Some international visitors come just for Carnival, Brazil's biggest party of the year. Carnival takes place over three days before Lent in February and is an important event in every Brazilian's calendar. For some, it takes the rest of the year to get ready for the next one. Community groups in the poorer neighborhoods of Rio have their own *samba* schools with up to 6,000 members. Each *samba* school chooses its own theme for costumes and writes a song to perform during Carnival. *Samba* schools compete against each other to become the Carnival champions alongside thousands of musicians, actors, and storytellers who also take part in the celebrations.

▼ During Carnival, the rhythm of samba drums continues day and night.

CHAPTER 13

Environment and Conservation

The Amazon basin is teeming with life, especially high above the ground in the forest canopy. Here, trees flower all year, and monkeys and animals such as sloths can find plenty of seeds and fruits to eat. On the forest floor below, the hot, humid climate rapidly breaks down dead plants and leaves. This rotting material releases nutrients that are absorbed by tree roots to be recycled for more growth. Thanks to this constant cycle of growth and decay, trees such as the kapok can grow up to 200 feet (60 meters) high. Some nutrients are lost in the rainwater that drains into the Amazon River and its tributaries. These nutrients provide food for up to 2,000 types of fish, including the piraracu which can grow up to 13 feet (4 m) long.

EXHAUSTED SOIL

For decades, human activity has put the Amazon environment under pressure. Many poorer Brazilians have moved into the Amazon to clear land to grow food for their families. Cattle ranching, however, is the leading cause of deforestation in the Brazilian Amazon. The number of cattle in the Amazon doubled during the 1990s, but when ranches replace the forest, the soil is quickly exhausted. Some people say the cleared lands become like a desert after just ten years. Tropical rain forest soils are not fertile to begin with, but without falling leaves from the trees, the soils lose their only source of nutrients. Farmers sometimes add chemical fertilizers to boost the soil's fertility, but they are fighting a losing battle.

POLICING THE AMAZON

Today, 20 million people live in the Amazon region, and new roads such as the BR163 are opening up frontiers for cattle ranchers, loggers and soy bean farmers. The Brazilian

▶ An area of Amazon rain forest is burned and cleared to make way for another soy bean farm. Ash and cinders act as a fertilizer for the land, but they are a poor substitute for the natural systems that they replace.

Environmental and Conservation Data

📁 Forested area as % total land area: 47.9

📁 Protected area as % total land area: 18

📁 Number of protected areas: 1,197

SPECIES DIVERSITY

Category	Known species	Threatened species
Mammals	394	81
Breeding birds	686	114
Reptiles	648	22
Amphibians	681	6
Fish	471	17
Plants	56,215	381

Source: World Resources Institute

Environment Agency (IBAMA) keeps a check on forest destruction. With such a vast area to police, IBAMA's job is very difficult, but a new hi-tech surveillance system is making a difference. Six satellites and eighteen aircraft now give a more accurate picture of how much forest is being cleared, and 900 patrol stations across the Amazon are equipped with telephones and computers to catch people who are clearing forest illegally. Destruction of the rain forest, however, has actually accelerated in recent years. More than 9,000 square miles (24,000 sq km) of forest was cleared in 2004. That's nearly 2,000 square miles (5,000 sq km) more than five years earlier. A growing demand for Brazilian soy beans from farmers in Europe and China, where the soy beans are used as animal feed, may explain the reversed trend. The news in 2005 is more promising, however, because there are signs that forest destruction is slowing down. Falling soy bean prices have discouraged farmers from clearing more forest, and the policing efforts of IBAMA are beginning to achieve some success.

▲ IBAMA employs thousands of park wardens to keep a check on activities that may harm the precious forest environment.

 Did You Know?

The Amazon has lost 220,000 square miles (570,000 sq km) of rain forest, an area almost as big as California and Florida combined. This amounts to about 15 percent of the Amazon's original forest cover.

THE KING OF THE FOREST

The Atlantic forest is Brazil's most threatened environment. Less than one-tenth of the original forest remains, and, as a result, one of Brazil's most beautiful animals is threatened with extinction. The golden-headed lion tamarin is nicknamed "the king of the forest" because its golden fur looks like a lion's mane. This small monkey uses its slender fingers to catch insects in the air and its strong fingernails to dig out tasty grubs hidden beneath the bark of a tree. In colonial times, a golden-headed tamarin was a favored pet for rich Europeans. Since then, these animals have been hunted for their silky coats and much of their forested home has been destroyed. There may be only 200 left in the wild. In the hope of saving the tamarin, some have been moved to protected areas of forest big enough for them to find a partner to breed in safety.

PROTECTED STATUS

National parks help to preserve some of Brazil's precious environments. Forty national parks cover about 5 percent of the country. Brazil is also taking steps to meet its commitments to reduce biodiversity loss. Nine hundred more areas, besides the national parks, were given special protection status in 2004. They cover

Focus on: Parrot Pressure

The Pantanal grasslands are one of the last refuges of the Hyacinth Macaw, the world's largest parrot. These parrots nest only in *manduvi* trees, in holes previously carved by woodpeckers. The beautiful plumage of the Hyacinth Macaw is highly prized, however, and just one of these birds is worth up to U.S.$10,000 on the black market. Meanwhile, *manduvi* trees are being cut down, leaving these magnificent birds fewer places in which to find a home.

▶ An adult Hyacinth Macaw is about 3 feet (100 centimeters) long, and its loud squawks can be heard more than half a mile (1 km) away. Only 3,000 Hyacinth Macaws remain in the wild, and almost all of these are found in Brazil.

every type of environment, including 950,000 square miles (2.5 million sq km) of Amazon rain forest, and 170,000 square miles (450,000 sq km) of Atlantic forest.

SAVING THE TURTLES

Scientists are making efforts to protect the wildlife that inhabits Brazil's marine environment. On a beautiful beach called Praia do Forte in the northeast, Projeto (Project) Tamar is trying to save five species of sea turtles from extinction. A 37-mile (60-km) stretch of coastline is patrolled to stop people from stealing turtle eggs buried in the sand. Many of the eggs are carried carefully to a special incubation tank at Tamar's headquarters. Here, local people and tourists can watch the baby turtles hatch in safety and get a close-up view of some of their older relatives. Tamar's staff are mostly fishermen and their families. In the past, these same families may well have eaten the eggs.

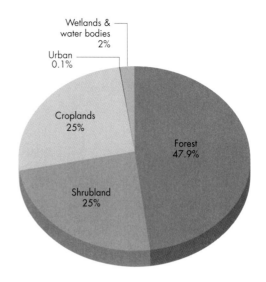

▲ Types of habitat

Did You Know?

Only 3 percent of Brazil's Atlantic Forest and about 11 percent of its Amazon rain forest is currently protected or set aside for sustainable uses.

▼ Once they have reached a certain size, baby turtles at Tamar's headquarters are released back into the sea.

CHAPTER 14

Future Challenges

Compared to the rest of South America, Brazil's economy is in good health and continues to attract investment from outside. The country still has a rich supply of resources, and more than 770,000 square miles (2 million sq km) of land could be used for farming in the future. Yet Brazilians face a challenge. In order to create jobs for the growing number of young

▼ At the Chico Mendes Brazil nut processing factory, a woman sorts and shells nuts that will be used in muesli and other products around the world.

people and to raise the standard of living for the millions of Brazil's poor, there is a danger that they may use up the natural resources on which they depend. People in other countries have to take some responsibility for the destruction of Brazil's natural resources. Illegally logged timber furnishes homes and offices elsewhere, and following health scares over European cattle herds, more Europeans now eat Brazilian beef from cattle ranches on land cleared in the Amazon basin. What's more, Brazil's debt repayments to overseas banks leaves less money to spend on projects that are sustainable and which help people find a way out of poverty.

A QUESTION OF BALANCE

The past offers lessons on how to find a lasting balance between satisfying people's needs and protecting the environment. The Central Amazonian Corridor in Amazonas state could be a model for the future. Created in 1997, reserves were joined together to cover an area of 22,000 square miles (570,000 sq km), the world's largest single area of protected rain forest. Here, farmers are learning ways of using the forest without cutting it down, much like their Amerindian ancestors. Growing fruit and nuts and harvesting rubber makes money, and unlike cattle ranching, these types of farming leave the forest intact for future generations.

PEACE AT LAST?

Land distribution is another important challenge because competition for land continues to lead to conflict and violence. Listening to the demands of the Landless Workers Movement (MST), the Brazilian government promised in 2003 to distribute some of Brazil's vacant land to 430,000 landless families by the end of President Lula's term in office. The MST argues that progress is too slow. By 2005, only 60,000 families had been resettled. The assassination of US-born missionary Dorothy Strang may quicken the pace of change. Sister Dorothy campaigned for more than thirty years for the land rights of poor farmers in Pará state. Anger and shock across Brazil over her brutal murder in February 2005 may mark a turning-point toward more peaceful solutions to land conflicts.

▲ Young Brazilians from all backgrounds are proud of their country. Modern Brazil offers them many opportunities for a prosperous future.

Despite these challenges, many Brazilians are very upbeat about their country's future. They are confident that Brazil will gain greater respect from the rest of the world, perhaps from groundbreaking technologies made and developed in Brazil or from its strengthening of alliances with other industrializing countries, particularly China and India. What's more, with the likely growth of the tourism industry, more people will learn about the amazing diversity of the country's attractions. This way, Brazil will be recognized and appreciated for more than just football, coffee, and Carnival!

Time Line

10,000 B.C. The likely arrival of the first peoples to settle in Brazil.

3,000 B.C. The beginning of Tupí-Guaraní, one of the main Amerindian languages in Brazil.

A.D. 1494 Spain and Portugal sign the Treaty of Tordesillas that gives Portugal control over Brazil.

1500 Portuguese explorer Pedro Álvares Cabral lands on Brazilian shores at Porto Seguro to begin nearly 300 years of Portuguese rule.

1695 Gold is discovered in Minas Gerais state.

1822 Pedro, the son of the Portuguese king, becomes Emperor of Brazil and rules Brazil as a monarchy.

1831 Pedro II becomes the second Emperor of Brazil. He remains in power for fifty-eight years.

1888 Slavery is finally abolished after almost 300 years. Many European immigrants move to Brazil to work.

1889 The monarchy is abolished, and Brazil becomes a republic with its own president.

1930 Getúlio Vargas seizes power in a coup, and rules Brazil as a dictator for fifteen years.

1958 A young Pelé stuns the world in the Soccer World Cup in Sweden. The seventeen-year-old scores six goals, including two in the final, enabling Brazil to beat the hosts and win the World Cup for the first time.

1960 Brasília becomes Brazil's new capital city.

1964 The government is overthrown by a military dictatorship.

1970 Brazilians begin building the Trans-Amazonian Highway.

1984 The Landless Workers' Movement (MST) begins.

1985 The military government finally gives up power, and people are again allowed to vote for their leader.

1988 A new constitution gives greater freedom and rights to ordinary Brazilians.

1992 Rio plays host to the world for the first Earth Summit. President Collor resigns after charges of corruption.

1994 Fernando Henrique Cardoso is elected president. He is the first president to stay in power for two terms.

2002 Lula da Silva begins his first term as president, and Brazil wins the Soccer World Cup for a record-breaking fifth time. Ronaldo scores both goals in a 2-0 defeat of Germany.

2003 Brazilian movie *City of God* wins worldwide critical acclaim and is nominated for four Academy awards. The movie is a true story of a young man who grew up in Cidade de Deus, a poor suburb of Rio de Janeiro.

2004 The first ever recorded hurricane in the south Atlantic strikes southern Brazil. With wind speeds of up to 90 miles (145 km) per hour, hurricane Catarina kills three people and leaves thousands of others homeless.

Glossary

alliance a group of countries, or other groups, that work together

Amerindian sometimes known as native Americans, descendants of people who lived in North or South America before the Europeans arrived

animist a belief in spirits that inhabit the natural world

archaeologist someone who studies the remains of ancient civilizations

Atlantic forest a type of forest that grows along Brazil's mountainous Atlantic coast

caiman a member of the alligator family

cerrado tropical grassland, known as savanna in other parts of the world

colony a country taken over and controlled by another

constitution an agreed set of rules and laws

deforestation the clearance of trees from land that was once covered by forest

dictator a powerful ruler of a country who makes most of the rules him or herself

eco-tourism often organized in small groups, eco-tourism aims to offer people the opportunity to experience natural environments and traditional cultures without damaging them

equatorial the climatic and environmental conditions of places that lie on the equator

evangelical part of the Protestant church that founds its teaching on the gospel

favelas poor neighborhoods or shanty towns in Brazil's towns and cities

fossil fuel types of energy sources, such as oil, coal, and gas, that are formed by fossilized plants and animals. They release carbon when they are burned.

gradient the steepness of the land, or the steepness of the fall of water

immigrant a person who moves from one country to settle in another

inflation an increase in the general level of prices

irrigation the artificial watering of land to help crops grow. It is normally practiced in areas of low or unreliable rainfall.

Lent the forty days before the religious holiday of Easter, when traditionally Christians fast, pray, and give money to the poor

malaria a tropical disease transmitted to people by mosquito bites

malnutrition a deficiency in the nutrients that are essential for the development and maintenance of the body

missionary someone who travels to places to convert people to his or her religion

nutrient minerals that plants use as food

plantation a type of farm found in tropical areas. A plantation usually covers a large area, and grows one or two types of crop.

plate part of the earth's crust

plateau a flat area of land on raised ground

republic a country that has a president rather than a king or queen as its head of state

river basin the area of land drained by a river and its tributaries

samba a Brazilian dance that originally came from Africa

sap watery liquid that flows through a plant

sedimentary rock rocks such as chalk, sandstone, clay, and carboniferous limestone formed by sediments laid down on the sea bed

smelting separating metal from a rock by melting it in extreme heat in a furnace

sustainable describes types of development that improve the quality of life for people by using resources carefully

trade winds tropical winds that blow toward the equator from the northeast (northern hemisphere) and the southeast (southern hemisphere)

tributary a river or stream that flows into another, usually larger, river or stream

várzea surrounding areas of land on the banks of the Amazon River that are flooded during the wet season

Further Information

BOOKS TO READ

Bowden, Rob. *Brazil* (Countries of the World). Evans Books, 2002.

Brimson, Samuel. *Brazil-East Timor* (Nations of the World). World Almanac Library, 2004.

Dalal, Anital. *Brazil* (Nations of the World). Raintree, 2004.

Green, Jen. *Rain Forests* (Young Scientist Concepts & Projects). Gareth Stevens, 1999.

McKay, Susan. *Brazil* (Festivals of the World). Gareth Stevens, 1997.

Morrison, Marion. *Rio de Janeiro* (Great Cities of the World). Gareth Stevens, 2004.

Parker, Edward. *The Amazon* (Great Rivers of the World). World Almanac Library, 2003.

Parker, Edward. *The Changing Face of Brazil.* Hodder Wayland, 2004.

Robinson, Roger. *Brazil* (Country Studies). Heinemann Educational, 1997.

Scoones, Simon. *A River Journey: The Amazon.* Hodder Wayland, 2003.

Scoones, Simon. *South America* (Continents of the World). Gareth Stevens, 2006.

USEFUL WEB SITES

www.ecobrazil.com
Provides information about tour packages in Brazil.

www.vivabrazil.com
Take a virtual trip through Brazil.

www.mongabay.com/brazil.html
Information and satellite images on forest destruction in the Amazon.

www.socioambiental.org/pib/english/indiandus/krenaki.shtm
Amerindian groups in Brazil.

http://forests.org/brazil
For the latest news articles about rainforest destruction and conservation.

www.survival-international.org
Survival International is a worldwide organization supporting tribal peoples, including Amerindian groups.

Web sites change frequently, and sometimes they become outdated or irrelevant to the topics they were initially designed to address.

For Web sites about Brazil that are current, informative, and appropriate to the subject, please visit our Web site at www.garethstevens.com/ and follow the links to World in Focus and Brazil.

Index

Page numbers in **bold**
indicate pictures.

About the Author

Simon Scoones is a tutor on the postgraduate teacher-training program at the Institute of Education/University of London. He is also the author of the www.globaleye.org.uk website for schools. He has taught Geography and Social Studies in the UK, and in international schools in Singapore and Antwerp, Belgium. He has written a number of books on environment and development issues for young people and is widely traveled across six continents.